Save Your Money, Save Your Life:

110 Ways to Cut Spending and Reach Financial Freedom

By James Conklin

Contents

Why Focus on Savings and Expenses? 3

Where Does It All Go? 5

Utility Savings 6

Saving Around the House 13

Food and Dining Savings 18

Finance Savings 34

Travel Savings 42

Health and Personal Care Savings 46

Saving with Kids 51

Saving with Infants 55

Automotive Savings 59

Entertainment Savings 67

General Shopping Strategies 71

Mental Shifts to Help You Save 74

Save Your Money, Save Your Life 76

Why Focus on Savings and Expenses?

In David Copperfield, Charles Dickens wrote, "Annual income twenty pounds, annual expenditure nineteen six, result happiness. Annual income twenty pounds, annual expenditure twenty pound ought and six, result misery."

His point, and it has been repeated in thousands of different ways, is that one of the great keys to happiness in life is gaining control of your expenses and having extra to save.

Your reasons to save are going to vary based on your goals in life and are going to vary over time. I've realized that over my life, my reasons for savings have made an evolution.

When I first started getting any kind of money (probably around age 8), I took on the philosophy of *spending soon*, but on the best of immediate choices. Sure, I wouldn't just spend on anything, but I would spend it pretty quickly on the best of the available options.

Getting a little older and wiser, I adopted the habit of *saving to spend*. Saving to spend means delaying immediate gratification and requires you to make choices on your expenses to allow you to save for things. You cut expenses and save for a new car, for a wedding ring, for a down payment on a house, for new toys, for fancy meals and for anything substantial. This is far better than living paycheck to paycheck and keeps you ahead of your expenses instead of being in debt and chasing them. The incentive to cut expenses here is to allow you to buy things that are of greater value in the future.

After we had a few kids and were years into a career, I recognized a third purpose to cutting expenses and to saving more.

This higher purpose has transformed my view on personal finance and my passion for reducing my expenses. My awareness of this greater purpose came as I read the book Your Money or Your Life by Vickie Robin and Joe Dominguez and started to pay attention to bloggers in the early retirement / financial independence movement. What these resources taught me is that beyond just saving to spend, the savings themselves could produce passive income and, more importantly, that if you could get that passive income high enough and your expenses low enough, you eliminate the need for your normal 9-5 job.

Dropping out of the normal 9-5 career path may seem on the surface like an impossibility before 65 (it certainly did to me) but it is not an out of reach goal for many if they are willing to adjust their lifestyle. The biggest influence on an individual's ability to gain financial freedom is not their income, it is the space between their income and their expenses. This realization gave me an increased desire to find ways to cut my family's spending and save our money for a future where our money can work for us, not just have us work for it.

Whatever your reasons for saving money, I hope some of these ideas will spark you to learn more and put them into action. Saving money won't feel like a chore when you remember what your purpose is!

Where Does It All Go?

In 2009, the US Bureau of Labor Statistics provided a detailed look on how the average US consumer spends their paycheck. The results were revealing and illustrate the areas where there is usually the most room in a family's budget to cut back. The average family expenditure of $49,638 had the top categories of
1) Housing - 34.1% (Includes shelter, utilities, household supplies and furnishings)
2) Transportation - 17.6% (Includes the cost of vehicles, fuel, and other expenses)
3) Food - 12.4% (Includes food at home and away)
4) Insurance and social security - 10.8%
5) Healthcare - 5.7%
6) Entertainment - 5.4%

In this book, I've tried to highlight some of the ways that you can reduce expenses and save money in these and other categories. Some of these ideas are nudges in behavior, others require specific steps either called out or that can be found by searching online. Because of length and because individual situations will vary, these ideas are meant as jumping off points and motivation and not always the exhaustive set of instructions. Find the ideas that apply to you and put them to work. Whether you take a big bang approach or start with small cuts, I hope that these ideas will help you to reach your financial goals!

Utility Savings

Don't fight Mother Nature
Some households will keep their temperature in the summer at 68 degrees and winter temperature at 74. While it feels great to have such a large contrast from oppressive weather outside, it is also costing you a bundle. The Department of Energy recommends keeping your thermostat at 68 degrees in the winter and 78 in the summer. Whether or not you use a programmable thermostat, scale back your overall usage to these temperatures and save on one of your biggest monthly utilities bill.

Nearly Free Fires
While most houses are build with regional or forced air heating, wood is a much older and potentially much cheaper way to heat some or all of your house. We have a relative who for the last 10 years has had fires all winter long but has never once paid for wood. His creative wood sourcing has cut his heating bills to half of what they would have been if he had to rely completely on his furnace. The first step to making the most of wood power is ensuring you have an efficient wood stove or fireplace. A drafty fireplace will provide some warmth but a good stove will take less wood and provide more heat. Once you have your stove or fireplace, there are a number of creative ways to get wood on the cheap:
1) Gather as a service - One of the most reliable sources for this family member was gathering wood as part of helping people. Whether it was a fallen tree on someone's property or a stump that needed to be pulled, he would do them the benefit of removing it from their property and himself the benefit of turning it to firewood.
2) Use Craigslist - Craigslist and other local classifieds can also be a good source of free wood. Whether it is someone moving and needing to get rid of a store of wood or someone wanting you to remove their

tree in exchange for the wood, if you have the tools and transportation there are probably lots of chances in your area

3) Harvest It Yourself - Some areas will allow you to cut your own firewood on public land if you have a permit. The permit is usually cheap and you can often take as much as you can load up.

4) Be Scrappy - If there are carpenters or other wood working business in your area they may have scrap piles that they would be happy to offload to you. You probably aren't going to get large slow-burning pieces but you may be able to pick up free boards and kindling.

Switch to LEDs

With LEDs, Compact Fluorescent (CFL), and Incandescent bulbs all on the market, customers can be a bit overwhelmed at all the lighting choices. When you look beyond the initial cost per bulb (where incandescent bulbs always win) though, LEDs come out as a clear winner for savings. The website eartheasy.com presents a cost comparison table for LEDs vs CFL vs Incandescent Bulbs. From this table the cost for 50,000 hours of usage (including the purchase price) puts LEDs at $85.75, CFLs at $89.75, and incandescent at $352.50. As if that wasn't enough incentive, it actually gets even better. Many utility companies offer substantial rebates for energy efficient bulbs. In the Seattle area for example, rebates on LED bulbs take their cost down to $5.00 or less at Costco and Home Depot. This would put your total cost for 50k hours (or 4.5 years at 6 hours a day) of LED usage to $54.80, which is a $297.70 savings over incandescent for that period! Multiply that by the number of bulbs in your house and you get to some pretty huge savings..

Make Hot Water Washes the Exception

You've got a lot of options on your washer but that doesn't mean that the simplest, cold wash/cold rinse, isn't the best. While hot water will do a better job of killing bacteria and removing stains, for most loads of laundry, it simply isn't worth it. Washing in cold water makes for less wear and tear on your clothes, and is way, way less expensive. In a study done by personal finance blog, The Simple Dollar, a load of hot wash/warm rinse cost $0.68 per load where a load of cold/cold cost just $0.04. If you are doing 6 loads a week and can reduce your hot washing to just one of them, that could save you over $150 per year.

Indoor/Outdoor Clotheslines

The second highest energy consumer for most families is the dryer and, unlike the #1 consumer (your fridge), is pretty easy to reduce your usage. Air drying your clothes, either indoor or out, doesn't give you as quick of a turnaround time or, in our experience, the softness of tumble-dry, but it does have a number of benefits. Number one is the cost - drying without a dryer can save $120 a year if you are doing 400 loads/year. Another benefit is the sanitizing power of the sun if you are able to dry outside. The aforementioned time cost is a concern, as is the unsightliness of airing your laundry but if it works for you, take this easy route to reducing your energy bill.

Stop Renting Your Modem

Cable companies are more than happy to rent you a cable modem for up to $8.00 per month (ie Comcast). Many consumers probably don't realize that they could get a modem that functions identically for as little as $40. That means that after just 5 months, your $40 investment is paid off and you are saving $8 every month and almost $100 per year. Installing an internet modem is an operation any novice can perform (just plug in 3 wires, you can't get it wrong), the only minor hookup may be a call to your cable company to recognize and activate it. Very few investments are this easy or quick to pay off, don't let another month go by paying your internet provider more than you already are.

Slow the Flow

During the summer months, water and electricity go hand in hand as the highest utility bills for most families. Finding ways to reduce water consumption during summer and year-round can make a big difference in your bill, particularly if you are in a dry area that has tiered water utility pricing. Some ways to reduce your water usage include:

1) Turn off the water while you are brushing your teeth. If you brush for the two minutes your dentist recommends, you don't need two minutes worth of water.

2) Consider a low-flow toilet. A dual-flush toilet or putting a filler (ie a brick in a waterproof container) in the tank can reduce the cost-per-flush.

3) Water only at in the early morning. Most homeowners are aware of this but make morning (4 AM to 10 AM) the time you water. Watering at night can leave the water sitting on the soil and cause fungal issues. Watering during the day leads to water wasted due to evaporation.

4) Consolidate your washing. Whether it is your dishwasher or your washing machine, unless your washer has a sensor then you are going to be using close to the same amount of water and running fewer, larger loads will be more efficient. There is, of course, a limit to this - you want to make sure what you are washing actually gets clean, but find the maximum size that works for you.

5) Harvest the rain. Rain barrels and other rain harvesting systems can be a great way to reuse free rain water for a garden or yard. There is an upfront investment and they don't always look great but once you have it in place, you'll appreciate being able to make use of free water!

Reduce Garbage Service

While you probably aren't going to be able to get rid of garbage collection, you can cut it down to the bare minimum if you put some effort into it. First, you'll have to reduce your consumption. Whether it is buying products with less packaging or just generally buying less, having less coming into your house is going to mean less going out. Second, recycle everything you can. You probably have recycling collection as readily available as garbage in your area (and for many areas, it is included in the cost of garbage) and you usually have a much larger bin. Once we made recycling a priority, we realized that we were recycling far more than we were throwing away. The third piece to cutting down your garbage service is to find a way to get rid of food and green waste. Some areas offer composting or yard waste collection services. Other families will have large enough yards or access to green areas where they can dispose of compostable waste. Between composting and recycling, you should have a pretty minimal amount that actually is going to the landfill. In our area, the difference between the large 64-gallon pickup and the small, 20-gallon container is nearly $40 a month. Over a year, cutting down on waste would not only be good for the Earth but could save you nearly $500.

Drop the Land Line

In a family where every member of the household has a cell phone, do you really need a landline? For many families, the answer is no. With cell minutes plentiful, Skype calls free, and land lines often filled with additional taxes, fees, and unused services, dropping it makes a lot of financial sense. There are some downsides though if you had a traditional land line - if power AND cell towers went down, you would have a harder time getting a hold of anyone. With a land line, you also don't usually have to worry about lost or uncharged phones when you are just plugged into the wall. Although there is some mental comfort in having a landline, it comes at a steep price. We've been landline free for more than five years and have never looked back. With the savings over $200 a year, we aren't likely to change that anytime soon.

Shop Around for Cell Service

Cell service providers are getting more competitive all the time and there are far more options available to customers than there were even just a couple years ago. At the high end are prices as high as $250 for a traditional family plan from AT&T. At the mid tier, you can find services like T-Mobile's family plan which runs $110 for 5 lines, which isn't too bad for a per-line price. If you are just looking for one or two lines and are not an extreme user, there are some great new options that can save you even more. One of them, Republic Wireless, offers a plan with unlimited talk and text and some data (read the small print) for just $10 a month after you buy a compatible phone (as low as $99). They have plans even cheaper ($5 if you only use WiFi), and others that give you faster speed but for a significant amount more. If you can't give up your iPhone, T-Mobile has a $30 plan that includes unlimited talk, text, and data. None of these plans are going to include the cost of your phone but when you look at the cost over a few years, you'll definitely come out ahead.

Take Advantage of Free Utility Offerings

Utilities, either out of city mandates, advertising, or good will, often have a number of free products or services that aren't always well advertised. Visit your utility's website (it will be on your bills) to learn about some of their programs. Some easy ones to take advantage of are:

1) Energy Reduction kits - Many utility companies offer water/energy reduction kits for residents in their area and all you have to do is fill out a form online. We took advantage of this and in the kit came 2 faucet flow reducers (little caps you screw into a sink faucet to reduce the water flow and increase aeration), a low-flow shower head and 2 compact fluorescent light bulbs. These all came at no cost to us and are going to save us money in the future.

2) Lighting discounts - In our area, there are instant rebates available on CFL and LED light bulbs available right at the hardware store that reduce the cost by more than 50%. This makes buying local way less expensive than ordering online and are a good way to save long term.

3) Energy Star rebates - If you are making major purchases, look for programs offered by your state, city, or utility company. Anything that is going to put a major dent in your energy usage (washers, dryers, fridges, solar panels, hot water heaters, new windows, etc) may have a sizable rebate that can ease the upfront cost of these investments. We have taken advantage of this with our washer and dryer (saved $100 off the combined $700 purchase), and factor in these rebates as part of any new purchase we consider.

4) Energy Audits - Energy audits may be offered for free or at a low cost and provide an inspection of areas that your home may be wasting energy. In most cases, this will be in areas like insulation gaps and if investments here could pay off in 3 - 5 years, they are probably going to be worth it.

Saving Around the House

Dishwasher Detergent Decisions
If you are like most families, you run your dishwasher at least once a day and if you are paying as much as $0.28 for a detergent tab per load, you'll spend right around $100 per year just on detergent. One option to reduce this cost would be to make your own dishwasher detergent. The website houselogic.com has a comparison of 7 different recipes that all come out to be about $0.05 or less per load. Our family tried a couple of different recipes and in the end, couldn't find one that did as great of a job as store-bought detergent. Maybe for us it was the water or the specific recipe we used but we found there was a slight residue left on some of our plastic dishes. We decided to abandon do-it-yourself and ended up saving by looking for sales and by not using more detergent than was necessary. By following this method, we usually end up buying liquid or powder that costs $0.10 per load and while that is more expensive than a homemade solution, is far less than individual tablets or full-price brand-name options.

Make your own Laundry Detergent
While we didn't find success with making our own dishwasher detergent, we had better luck with making washing detergent. The internet is full of recipes but for us, a combination of soap, borax, and washing soda seemed to get the job done at about a third of the cost of commercial detergent. We tried both liquid and powder recipes and while they both seemed effective at cleaning clothes, the powder formula left soap residue on the inside of the washer. With a liquid recipe, the only downside has been the larger storage requirement to store our non-concentrated mixture.

The recipe we follow is

1) Take a bar of soap (doesn't have to be anything fancy) and shred it using a food processor.
2) Heat 2 quarts of water and add the soap you just shredded. Keep stirring until the soap is dissolved.
3) In a 5-gallon bucket (home depot has them pretty inexpensively), combine 4.5 gallons of hot tap water, 1 cup of washing soda, 1 cup of Borax, and the soap mixture you made in (2). We also like to add in some essential oils but that is totally optional. Our favorite is a mix of ~20 drops of Lavender and 20 drops of Orange. Stir this all together.
4) Cover and let it cool overnight
5) Stir again to make sure it is smooth and consistent and then transfer to more convenient containers. We like to use old juice and milk containers after they have been cleaned out.

Just half a cup of this mix is plenty for us and costs well under $0.10 per load.

One additional idea - if you want a fabric softener, consider replacing your traditional fabric softener with white vinegar which will cost far less ($1.50/gallon) and will still leave your clothes feeling soft and fresh.

Wash Not Waste
It took us a long time to find a hand dish washing solution that worked for us. We tried sponges but they didn't last long before they got a smell and bristle brushes didn't last too long either. We got tired of the expense of replacing them (and the hassle of running out) but found success when we switched to small dish cloths that we would use one per day and then wash them all with the rest of our laundry at the end of the week. We found a similar approach worked well with paper towels. Rather than always reaching for a paper towel and then throwing it away, we use one of our cloths that we wash regularly. We haven't gone so far as replacing paper napkins yet but many families use cloth napkins with success. Because the effect on your regular

wash is minimal, there is very little marginal cost and you can save yourself the expense and hassle of buying a lot of paper and cleaning products.

Be Aware on Repairs

The cost and quality of home repairs and renovations can vary more than just about any other service we pay for. Whether it is a plumbing leak or an electrical project all the way up to a remodel or room addition, it is easy to feel out of control when you can't get prices up front and you aren't an authority on the quality of work. To save yourself from emotional and financial pain, we've found a few tips that help:

1) Look for well reviewed companies - Picking the first company from the Yellow Pages is so last century. It used to be that the only source of recommendations were people you knew and if you couldn't get a referral there, you had to pick blindly from a phone book. With the internet and customer reviews, you now have a lot more information at your fingertips. For small jobs, we typically will just go with free sites like Yelp or Google+ and looks for high and consistent reviews of service providers. For larger jobs, we look harder to find referrals from people we know and have found that pay sites like Angie's List can be worth it for really large projects.

2) Check the credentials - Verifying that your service provider is licensed, bonded, and with the Better Business Bureau can give you at least a glimmer of hope for recourse if things go wrong.

3) Get multiple bids - When even a plumbing repair can cost hundreds of dollars, it pays to get multiple bids. Getting at least 3 bids for significant work can help make you more of an expert on the pricing and options of different providers. When we needed to replace a set of windows for a condominium, the prices ranged from $5500 up to $7000 between 3 bidders. In the end, we found a coupon that reduced a $6500 bid down below $6000 for the company we trusted most.

Fix It Yourself

Growing up, for my family and many others, we didn't tackle a lot of repairs ourselves. Part of this was a lack of easily accessible information (you could probably look up repairs at a library or buy a book but that took a significant amount of searching) but part of what was lacking was the feeling of empowerment to try to fix it ourselves even though it 'wasn't our job'.

Something that we have now adopted and is a great way to gain skills and to save money is to at least investigate fixing issues around your house and with your vehicles prior to calling in a professional. Whether it is plumbing issues like fixing a leak (buy a replacement pipe connection and plumbers putty), unclogging a drain (buy a $15 pipe snake on Amazon), or unjamming a disposal (resetting breakers, cleaning, then forcing the motor with the manual lever), we were able to search online and solve these problems ourselves. Beyond plumbing, we have solved car issues with just a set of zip-ties (this was for something that wasn't safety critical!) that we would have spent hundreds at an auto shop and we have also learned to patch drywall and to do our own painting which we otherwise would have had to contract out. We wouldn't feel comfortable tackling anything structural or electrical or that could pose a safety risk without more consultation but we have saved a great deal, and gained a great deal of empowerment, by learning and applying ourselves to problems around the house.

Landscaping Solutions

While there is nothing quite like watching kids play on a nice green lawn or laying in the grass to look up at the stars, a large green grassy lawn could be costing you in a number of different ways. With average lawn care prices starting at $35-$45 a visit, you could be spending over a thousand dollars over the course of a summer on maintenance. When you add to that the cost of watering and fertilizing you reach a pretty significant figure if you want a hands-off grass experience. The obvious first step to cutting down in this area is to get the exercise and handle the job yourself. It will take a few hours out of your weekend but you'll keep the grass without the maintenance cost.

Beyond that though, consider replacing some (or all) of your grass with options that are less maintenance or that give back. If you still want a green spread, there are alternatives to traditional grass that take less care and less water like Blue Star Creeper or Sheet Moss or Clover (though watch out for the bees it attracts).

You could also consider artificial grass which doesn't look as bad as you would think, takes no water, and is pretty durable. If you are willing to get more creative, check out either landscaping with stone or planting a variety of plants that will look good and return fruits or vegetables. If you are looking for a low-maintenance, low-water space, research Permaculture which is a land design philosophy modeled around self maintaining habitats.

Charge and Re-charge

Between remote controls, flashlights, toys, baby monitors, video game controllers, tools, and other devices, many families can chew through batteries at a pretty quick pace. For around $50 on Amazon, you can buy a battery charging kit like the La Crosse Technology BC1000 Alpha Power Battery Charger that will allow you to recharge nicd and nimh AA and AAA rechargeable batteries and comes with 4 AA and AAA batteries to get you started. If you don't use batteries that often, this obviously isn't going to help you but if you never seem to have batteries on hand or go through a lot, this device can pay for itself in a year or two. Once the device is paid off with your savings, the only ongoing cost is the tiny cost of the electricity to recharge the drained batteries.

Food and Dining Savings

Repurpose Your Leftovers
If you've ever watched the TV show Chopped you've seen the masterpieces that professional and semi-pro chefs can do with a random set of ingredients. Take some inspiration from that and see what you can do with your own leftovers. Tacos one night and curry the next? Curry tacos coming right up! Make a roast but can't finish it? Use the beef and potatoes in a stew or repurpose the beef for nachos or a shepherd's pie. Leftovers get a bad wrap for being boring but by putting a new twist on some perfectly good food you can save yourself money on your grocery bill.

Take Your Lunch To Work
It's not uncommon for people to spend $10 or more on a workday lunch and if you are spending that every workday of the year, you're probably spending a few thousand per year on lunches. If you can live with a little repetitivity, the incremental cost of making extra the night before and packing leftovers is usually minimal. If you don't have a way to reheat a meal then sandwiches, fruits, nuts, and yogurt are also cost-effective options to reduce your per-day expenses.

Dried Beans Are Your Friend
Sure, a can of beans probably only costs you $1.00 but you can improve on that in a number of ways if you are willing to do some pre-planning and cook your own. Not only are dry beans much cheaper (about $0.40 per can after the cost of ingredients and the longer cooking time vs $1.00 for a store-bought can) but they also are going to allow you to have more control over the amount of sodium, you'll have less chemicals from sitting in a can for an undetermined amount of time, and, if you freeze them to reuse later, you have more control over portion size. Now how do you go about making use of dry beans? Pretty simple:

1) Rinse off the dry beans and remove any broken fragments.
2) Soak the beans overnight.
3) Put the beans in a pot and get up to boiling. Let it simmer until they are al-dente. For black beans, this is about an hour but may be longer depending on the type of beans and your altitude.
4) If you are going to use them that day, you are done, and can go ahead and incorporate them in your dish. Otherwise, drain the beans and you can spread them out on a cookie sheet, put that in the freezer for a few hours, then transfer to a freezer safe bag for later use.

If you use a can of beans a week, in addition to the health benefits you could save more than $30 a year.

Shop in Ethnic/Specialty Grocery Stores

If you've only ever shopped at traditional large grocery store chains, you might not realize there is a whole other world of grocery stores around you. The variety of ethnic and specialty grocery will depend largely on the ethnic makeup of your city but particularly if you are in a large city, you'll find a huge variety of Mexican, Asian, Middle Eastern, and other specialty stores. In these stores, you'll find a lot of selection that you won't find at your typical Safeway and you'll also see a lot of prices that will surprise you. Whether it is coconut milk or sushi rice, chicken legs to spices, you'll find the prices are frequently lower than traditional chains.

Eat Big at Happy Hours

Cutting out the happy hour drinks will certainly save you money but there is an upside to happy hours if you are able to slow down on too much booze. Using happy hours as a time to eat your meal can be a great money saving idea. Not only is this time of day usually less crowded but you can also fill up on cheap appetizers and eat a variety of foods for much cheaper than you would spend on an entree. Watch that you aren't just eating the fries though… that won't do your wallet or your waistline much good.

Put Your Garden To Work

Gardening isn't free and depending on what you already have, may have significant start-up costs to get the soil and tools you need. Additionally, it will require a lot of time, water, seeds, and potentially fertilizer before you get any returns. Despite all of this though, if you are growing what you will eat, you will almost always be able to make a return on your investment both financially as well as in the physical and mental health benefits that gardening has been proven to bring. JD Roth of the blog Get Rich Slowly tracked all of the costs that went into his garden for a year and compared them to the cost of buying the food he grew in the grocery store. At the end of the season, the expenses totalled a bit over $300 but the cost to have bought the food at the grocery store was over $600. While your results may vary, some tips to keep in mind include:

1) Grow what you eat - No sense in growing something you will just want to give away or dread eating.

2) Understand your climate - If you are in the Northwest, grow berries that thrive on rain, not peppers that take hot and dry weather. If you are in an area with little rainfall, choose produce that isn't going to be water intensive.

3) Learn locally - Talk with friends and neighbors to find out what works for them. Even within the same region, there are differences in soil, in micro-climates, in pests, etc that can make a difference in how successful you will be.

4) Seed vs Sprout - Growing from sprouts can let you start a bit later and increase your chances of success but it is more costly. With as inexpensive as most seeds are, it may be worth planting early and testing your luck with seeds and falling back to sprouts if needed.

Cans Can

Growing up, I saw canned foods as something that gathered dust in my grandparents food storage and was usually older than I was. As I started being more aware of food and food prices, I started to realize the value in being able to safely and conveniently seal away food that you get at the peak of ripeness or the peak of cheapness to use for the future. Some of the lessons we've learned from a few years of canning include:

1) Only can what you are going to eat - It saves you no money to can something you will never crack the seal on unless you are just saving the can for the end of the world when you are desperate. Learn what foods your family regularly eats and stick with those.

2) Start small - We regularly use tomato sauce for pasta and other meals and had the great idea to use our home grown tomatoes, add in spices, and make a fantastic sauce. We had a bumper crop of tomatoes so made a giant batch of sauce and canned 8 jars of it. The sauce tasted great when we were first making it but once we started unsealing the jars a few months later, the taste and texture had changed and we found it to be pretty unsatisfying. If you are trying a new canning item, try small before you go big.

3) Look for jars that fit your needs - If you are going to go through the food slowly (ie sauce), consider using smaller jars to make sure the food doesn't go bad between when you unseal it and when you use it up.

4) Pounce on great prices - When you have the canning supplies and know what works for you, pounce when the price is right. We can regularly get apples (granted, we are in Washington) for $0.50 and will buy up to 80lbs for apple sauce. Some families could probably do 5 times that but stick with rule (1) and don't overdo it.

5) Label your lids - You aren't going to be resealing with the same lid so feel free to pull out a marker and label and date your products. If you find yourself getting to the next canning season and you still have last years items, it may be time to reconsider how much you should be storing.

Optimize Your Organic Spending

How much more you are willing to spend for organic food is something that varies for each family but for most, going organic for everything is not affordable or not worth it. Being smart about which organic foods you buy and which traditional produce you buy can allow you to maximize your money while still allowing for you to reduce your pesticide intake. You have probably heard of the 'dirty dozen', a list of suggested foods to buy organic but there is also a 'clean fifteen', a set of foods you should consider skipping the organic route for. You can look up the full lists but the list of decent non-organic choices includes pineapples, avocados, and mangoes (many of these are skinned fruits where you don't eat the skin). On the high-pesticide list where you may want to consider organic are items like apples, strawberries, grapes, and celery. Balancing out your organic purchases will save you money and let you feel good about the food choices you are making.

Cut down on Juice
Fruit juice tastes good and has plenty of vitamin C but is extremely high in sugar (often equivalent to the same amount of soda) and has none of the fiber or other benefits of whole fruit. Save yourself some health and cost benefits by cutting down on juice or, if you want to stretch it out, water it down or drink it with a lot of ice. If you want the benefits of fruit and veggies, replace the juice with a real fruit smoothie. If you want to save money, just skip to the always healthy and practically free water.

Cook with a Crock Pot
Not only are crock pots one of the tastiest and and most convenient cooking methods, they are also one of the most inexpensive in a number of ways. From a guide put out by the City of Seattle, crock pots cost about $0.10 to run for 8 hours which beats just about every other heating device except the microwave. In addition to the energy savings, the low and slow cooking process can allow you to buy less expensive cuts of meat and still get them tender and flavor packed. Whether it is roast beef or chicken, a curry or a soup, regularly incorporating crock pot recipes in your rotation can save you time and money.

Group your Meals

According to a study by the Natural Resources Defense Council, Americans throw away 40% of the food they buy. With food being one of the top budget items for most families, cutting down on waste (and the amount of food bought in the first place) is a surefire way to save money.

One way to accomplish this is by grouping meals to make use of ingredients in multiple meals. By taking some extra time to plan out your week, you can make sure you are maximizing the food that you buy. When you know you are buying something that can't be consumed in a meal, look for other meals that could reuse that ingredient in some fashion. One example might be a whole chicken where you may roast it and have chicken with rice and vegetables on the first night but then can reuse the carcass and scraps for a chicken noodle soup. Another case we like to plan for is when we get a fresh bunch of green onions or cilantro. We wouldn't normally use them all for just one meal but if you plan ahead they make a great accent for a few meals during a week. If you can cut down the amount of waste to even half the average, that would save your family over $1,000 a year.

Make your own bread

Bread is ubiquitous and even with a breadmaker it will take a bit of time to put the ingredients together. Why make your own then? For one, if you take out the cost of labor (and many people don't mind the effort to bake), it is absolutely going to be cheaper. Adding up the cost of ingredients and energy will put the cost of making your own bread around $0.50 for the most basic up to $1.00 if you are using organic flour, milk, butter, etc. Compare that to a grocery store with $1.00 for the cheapest up to $5.00 for a loaf you'd feel better about eating. Swapping out that loaf of higher-end bread could easily save you more than $150 per year. In addition to the cost savings, there is also the benefit of controlling exactly what goes into your bread. Looking at the ingredient list of that $1.00 loaf of bread you'll see high fructose corn syrup and a list of preservatives a mile long. Avoiding that will be good for your health *and* pocketbook.

We spent years looking for the perfect recipe that had whole wheat, a not-too-dense texture, a bit of sweetness and a distinctive crust. Although the result was one that was not completely handled in a bread machine, we preferred the oven baked crust and we use a doubled recipe to reduce the amount of repeated work. We also found that the kind of flour mattered quite a bit - our best results were with a home-ground combination of white and red wheat. If store bought whole wheat is too dense, consider substituting a little bit of white. After a lot of experimentation, our favorite bread-maker based recipe is this:

Double Honey Whole Wheat Bread

Combine in a large (ie Zojirushi) bread maker in order:
1 1/2 cup warm water
6 tablespoons honey
1 egg
3 tablespoons butter
1 scant teaspoon salt
1/2 cup vital wheat gluten
4 1/2 cups fresh whole wheat flour
1 heaping tablespoon yeast

Let this run on your bread machine's dough setting.
When that is finished, remove from the bread machine and form into two loaves (if you've never formed a loaf, we simply cut the dough in half and shape it into two oval pieces that would fit in bread pans). Place each loaf of dough into a greased bread pan. We find that either a greased cast-iron bread pan or else a Pyrex bread pan with parchment paper works best.

Let rise for 30 to 45 minutes while preheating the oven to 350 degrees fahrenheit.

Place into the oven and cook for 30 minutes.

After letting the loaves rest for 10 minutes, remove the loaves from the pans to let them cool. Add butter, jam, peanut butter or even enjoy it plain!

We typically will put one loaf in a freezer bag and freeze it (after it has gotten to room temperature) and eat the other one fresh over the next few days. When you are ready for the frozen loaf, just remove it and open the bag and it should be ready to eat in about 6 hours.

Coupon Smartly

As shows like Extreme Couponing and hundreds of blogs have shown, couponing can be an unhealthy obsession. At its worst, you have people spending a huge amount of time and end up going around buying things they don't actually need. Done right though, and couponing has the potential to save you money. Keep in mind:

1) Don't let coupons sway your decision on what to buy. Changing your purchase habits is exactly what coupons are meant to do but if you buy an additional item just to save with the coupon then you aren't actually saving money.

2) Value your time. While the "old-fashioned" route of clipping actual coupons from actual newspaper ads still works there are other alternatives that can be way faster. Grocery store programs like Safeway's Just4U can allow you to clip coupons right in your mobile app without the time spent scouring papers and cutting things out.

3) Actually remember the coupon. Before we switched to mostly digital coupons, our biggest problem was actually remembering the coupons at the register. If you have kids who are going berserk at the end of the trip and you see the shining sunlight of freedom, the last thing on your mind may be the coupons stuffed in your pocket. Either put the coupons in with your credit cards, go digital, or find some other way but don't forget to actually use the coupons when you get to the cashier.

Buy Generic

Buying generic or store brands can be another way to save money at the grocery store. Generic brands are often made by the same manufacturers that produce the national brands that you see but are often 20% or more less expensive. While we'll admit that there are some products we still prefer the name-brand for, generics are frequently worth it for us. Some of the areas we've found luck going generic include:

1) Infant Formula - The FDA inspects and mandates the ingredients and manufacturing of infant formula in the US and though the smell and taste may vary slightly, the health and quality won't be a difference with generics. The Costco store brand worked really well for our children and was one of the cheapest options we could find.

2) Cereal - For our family, cereal was hit or miss. For crispy rice, we had no problem with the generic brand but for toasted o's which you would think would be simple to replicate, we preferred the name brand.

3) Cooking Essentials - We haven't noticed any difference between brands for kitchen staples like salt, sugar, white vinegar, white flour, etc. With their simple ingredient lists, there just isn't much variability.

4) Juice - We didn't like store brand sodas but our main use of juice is in fruit smoothies and we didn't notice any difference in juices.

5) Water - Buying water is best avoided (see below), but when you have to, we couldn't tell any difference between brands. Water snobs probably can but I guess we aren't that sophisticated.

Reusable Water Bottles

The waste of plastic water bottles on the environment is huge and the waste on the wallet of spending money on water is also an almost always unnecessary expense. Particularly at specialty events (fairs, movies, sporting events), a simple bottle of water can run as high as $5.00! On average, Americans actually pay more per gallon for individually packaged bottled water than they do for gasoline! The $10 investment for a Nalgene bottle or other sturdy water container is going to pay for itself quickly and keep you from many kinds of waste. If you know there are going to be circumstances that you just can't avoid a consumable bottle, at least plan ahead and get a supply at Costco or another large retailer where you pay closer to $0.10 a bottle.

Make Your Own Broth
You could buy a can of chicken, vegetable or beef broth from a can at the grocery store and spend $1.00 - $2.00 for something extremely high in sodium and lacking in authentic taste. A little more labor intensive option would be to make your own broth where you control the ingredients and portion size for a much smaller cost. You can find recipes for beef and vegetable broths easily online but our favorite is a simple chicken broth that doesn't require us to buy any additional ingredients from what we already were going to throw out:
1) Store your vegetable trimmings in a sealed bag or other container in your freezer. Keep onion ends, carrot ends, unused celery stalks, etc.
2) Add all of your veggies and a chicken carcass or bony chicken pieces to a crock pot.
3) Let them cook in the crockpot for 6 hours on high (or simmer on the stove for 1-2 hours).
4) Strain the resulting broth and portion in a way that will be most convenient for you. For us, we typically use some of the broth immediately for soup but then also portion out the broth in freezer trays and freeze for future use.

Make Your Own Spice Packets
A pack of McCormick's spice mix can cost $0.99 - $2.99 from your grocery store shelves. Buying the same amount of spices in bulk and combining them yourself from a place like Winco will cost $0.20 - $0.40. Whether it is steak seasoning, taco seasoning, cajun seasoning or a mix of your own creation, you can save huge by buying spices in bulk. Buying your own small spice jars and using bulk to refill them will quickly be more efficient than buying pre-filled jars as well.

Choose U-Pick

There has been a resurgence recently in the number and availability of farms that allow customers to come and pick their own produce. This cuts out a number of middlemen (transportation to distributors, transportation to stores, storage, and store display) and allows the farmer to offer a much reduced price to pickers. We've been able to find fruits and vegetables for about half the grocery store price. Additionally, many of these U-Pick farms practice organic or near-organic (following organic practices but have not paid for certification) farming if that matters to you. All of these benefits do come with a cost - if you are in the city you'll probably have to make a bit of a drive to get to the farm and the picking itself will take as long as you're willing to spend. We've found the best success by taking the whole family, picking until the kids can't handle anymore, and then taking the fruit home to wash and freeze it. We make smoothies every day of the week and are able to get at least a third of our year's blueberries, raspberries and blackberries picked in just a couple of Saturday afternoons.

Farmers Markets

Farmers' Markets are becoming increasingly common even in urban settings. Farmers' Markets bring the benefits of fresh and known-source food without the hassle of a drive to the country. The produce isn't going to be as cheap as U-Pick but you can pick up a variety of fruits and vegetables much more easily and you can talk with the farmer about their farming practices. In our experience, the prices at the market are about 75% of the grocery store and the savings are even better when you are at the peak of the season. In addition to standard fruits and veggies, you can often find meats, jams, flowers and other not-from-a-factory products.

Know Your Prices

Prices for what you buy at grocery stores can vary greatly depending on what week you shop and at what store you shop at. With incomplete knowledge, it can be hard to know if the regular or sale price you are seeing is actually a good deal. One way to help this problem is to start keeping a simple price comparison book either in your phone or a physical notepad. By recording what prices you see for your most commonly purchased items at a few places that you regularly go to (for example, your primary and secondary grocery store, Costco, and Amazon), you'll have a good starting point to know what normal ranges are. Then, when you're doing your shopping, you will know if you are overpaying and should consider skipping that item or whether you are truly seeing a good deal and you should stock up.

Buy In Bulk

There are two different meanings to buy in bulk. One is the Costco approach where you are buying normal packaged goods in large quantities. This often has the advantage of cheaper prices but the disadvantage that you are committing to a large amount of storage space and a large amount of consumption. For products like toilet paper, storage bags, flour, etc, this shouldn't be a problem but may not be an approach apartment dwellers can easily adopt.

The other way to consider buying is the self-service bulk model where you get what you need and store in your own container. This often has a price advantage (you pay for no packaging, advertising, etc) and also has the advantage that you can get as much or little as you want. We like to buy many raw goods like wheat, nuts, and dried berries in this way to get the bulk savings but we also like to get small amounts of a variety of sweets because you can just get as much as you want for a movie, etc without leaving a ton lying around the house. If you are keeping a price book, you'll know how these prices compare to packaged goods and can recognize if stocking up in this way is right for you.

Squeeze out the Vices

Smoking, drugs, and excessive drinking, all the traditional vices, are not only poor to your health but, more relevant to our goal, are very expensive habits. Smoking a pack a day will cost in the neighborhood of $1700 per year. Drinking every day can also add up. Being selective about your use of these can not only liberate you from habits that restrict your freedom but also save you hundreds or thousands each year.

Shop with Preparation

Two preparations will help you to be a far smarter shopper at the grocery store. First, and well known, don't shop when you are hungry. When you are hungry, your willpower is lower and just about everything sounds tasty. Instead of looking for products that appeal on value or quality, you'll be more at the mercy of your easily distracted and hungry brain. Shopping after you've eaten will help you focus on getting what you really need. Second, shop with a list. If you have a list, you will be a far more efficient shopper as you will be less likely to forget things, less likely to buy things you don't need, and more likely to buy items you knew were on sale. A Wharton study found that, "People who consider themselves very "fast and efficient" shoppers are far less likely to make impulse buys — 82% less than the average." Go into the store prepared and then be efficient about making your purchases and you'll come out happy that you saved yourself from spending on unnecessary items.

Re-examine Daily Habits

For some people, it's a daily coffee. For others it's an afternoon cookie, soda, or vending machine purchase. Whatever it is, once it becomes a habit it can cost you in a number of ways. First of all is the cost. Spending $2.50 on a cup of coffee for 250 working days a year translates into $625 per year. While a treat every now and then is probably a good thing, are you consciously choosing to spend that much? Another benefit of stopping to re-examine your habits is the health and time benefits. Most things in moderation are fine but when it is a soda or three every single day, or a 30 minute detour in a coffee shop, the effects can add up. It's up to you to decide if it's worth it but make sure it is a conscious decision, not an expensive weight that you've unknowingly picked up.

Shop at Discount Grocers
If you only ever shop at a traditional grocery store, consider trying out a discount or fewer-frills store if you have one in your area. Discount retailers like Grocery Outlet and Save-A-Lot or no-frills grocers like Winco or Aldi's can provide significant discounts off what for many families is one of their highest bills. Both Winco and Aldi's are growing rapidly in the US and with good reason.
At Winco, an employee-owned store, not only are there rock bottom prices but their bulk foods selection is second to none. They have a fantastic selection of bulk spices, grains, nuts, and sweets that make shopping there fun as well as less expensive.
Aldi's takes a different approach than most grocers and stocks mostly it's own brand of products. This means that there is far fewer choices on the shelves and you won't be relying on the brands you have tasted before. This can be a good thing in a number of ways though. One benefit is the cost - we have seen Aldi's consistently be about 20% cheaper than comparable stores. Second is that this limited selection can limit impulse purchases. Because we know which Aldi's products we like and which we prefer other brands for, when we are at Aldi's we are able to stick with our plan and not do a lot of off-the-list shopping. While we don't love every single one of Aldi's products, we have found many that we like equal to or more than national brands. We also like their fantastic prices on produce. You might be intimidated by their deposit-required grocery carts or their brand-you've-never-heard of products but they are definitely worth a try and your budget will thank you.

Don't Make Meat Mandatory

I used to be of the philosophy that a meal wasn't a meal unless it had hot meat as a major part of it. A desire to save money as well as a desire to have more variety in our diet has opened our eyes to the benefits of going meatless some of the time. In addition to going meatless on some meals, we also have tried to make meat a complement to our meals rather than the dominant component. Things like soups with a little bit of leftover roast or chicken, nachos with pork scraps, or omelets with bacon bits, there are hundreds of dishes that won't feel lacking even if you tend to lean carnivore. Beans and other legumes are way cheaper than meat and can also be easily stored for the future so not only are you saving money but you are also giving yourself a future option in case of power outages, future job loss, or other cases where you need food on the shelf.

Eat In To Win
The US Department of Labor estimates that the average consumer spends over $2500 a year eating out. That figure is for an individual, if you are feeding a family, chances are it is quite a bit higher. Making eating out an exception rather than a frequent part of the week will make a huge difference in your expenses. Sure, eating out is convenient and often tasty but there are a few ways we've found to avoid eating out so frequently and spending so much.
1) Plan your meals ahead - One of the reasons we end up at restaurants is just not knowing what to cook for dinner. Making a meal plan will give you a concrete idea of what to make and keep you from heading to a restaurant out of indecisiveness.
2) Keep a backup - Another cause of restaurant temptation is a lack of easy options at home. To combat this, keep some freezer meals available that just require reheating. Even having soup on the shelf or some pasta and sauce available are enough to satisfy your family with very little effort.
3) Lower your standards - On Saturdays and Sundays, one thing we have found to be successful is to lower our dinner standards and get a bit creative. Some of our favorite weekend meals are traditional

breakfast meals - fruit and veggie smoothies with toast, pancakes, german pancakes, waffles, eggs, etc. These meals are different enough for us to feel kind of special but are super cheap, very easy, and keep us from eating out.

Restaurant Responsibly

If you do end up eating out, there are plenty of ways to do it and still feel alright about your spending levels. Some methods including
1) Splitting entrees - Better to come away from the meal not quite full and wishing for a little bit more than to eat more than you really wanted or leave wasted food on the plate. Pay half the price and feel better in a number of different ways.
2) Choose Kids Meals Carefully - Kids meals are a lot of fun but there are times that it is probably worth questioning them. If you are feeding a number of kids, would they get just as much food if you bought an entree and split it between them? Would they be just as happy if you split some appetizers between them and the family as a meal? Usually kids meals come with a lot of items you may not find worth it. If that's the case, look for alternatives.
3) Skip the drinks - Drinks can make up to 20% of the bill. If you are looking to save money, stick with water and buy the soda, juice, and wine elsewhere.
4) Order Online - If you are just looking for the food and not the ambiance, you can often save a lot of money ordering online. Many national chains have loyalty programs that will offer coupons, promotions for discounted or free food when you order online. Add to that the elimination of some of the gratuity and you'll end up spending less than if you dine in.

Finance Savings

Never Pay an ATM Fee

Before 1988, there were no ATM fees in the US but since then, they have become more common and more expensive. Nowadays, fees can range from $1.50 all the way up to a shocking $5.00 just to get some cash at an out of network machine. Your money should be making you money, not costing you even more money so make sure that you never (or nearly never) pay an ATM fee. Some strategies to avoid ATM fees include:

1) Withdraw in-network. Even if they aren't your primary banking institution, make sure you have a checking account connected to a large network of ATMs. That may be a nationwide bank (ie Chase, Bank of America) or a credit union that allows free withdrawals at other credit unions.

2) Get cash back. Instead of getting cash as a separate transaction, get cash back when you are getting gas, groceries, or other routine stops.

3) Get reimbursed. A number of banks including Charles Schwab will reimburse your ATM fees if you have to withdraw from out of network. Schwab even takes this a step further and will refund foreign ATM fees as well. All of that from a free checking account!

4) Skip cash altogether. The number of places you actually have to use cash is decreasing so skip the problem of having cash by saving it only for when you actually need it. Use credit or debit in all other cases.

5) If all else fails, reduce frequency. In most cases the fee won't change no matter how much you withdraw so if you absolutely have to make some withdrawals, reduce the number of times you are actually going to the ATM by getting out more cash each time. If carrying around that much cash is going to be a problem (either for physical safety or safety from your own spending) then see #4.

Never Pay a Finance Fee

The Wall Street Journal estimated that banks hauled in over $30 billion in overdraft fees in 2013 and that the median overdraft fee was $30. Paying an overdraft fee adds insult to injury and hurts people who can least afford to pay a hefty fee. One option is to pick an institution (such as a credit union) that will give you reasonable fees and control on whether or not to allow overdrafts. Some banks, such as Capital One 360 will charge you interest rather than a fee which is far cheaper, especially for small amounts. An even better option is to record (either on paper, mint.com, etc) your bank balance and outstanding charges to be sure you never hit the $0 point. Keep yourself from going further into the hole by always being aware of the amount you have available in the bank.

Make Credit Cards Work For You
Credit cards are a tool that can either work for you, or against you. All too common, credit cards are used to live beyond our means and end up costing a painful amount of interest. Hopefully by cutting your spending well below your income, you are avoiding that trap and once you have done that, you can then start to use credit cards responsibly and enjoy some of their many benefits. Credit cards, when used wisely, can offer a number of significant advantages over cash including:
1) Simple tracking of expenses. Whether you use a bank's website directly or an aggregator like mint.com, credit cards make it easy to see where you are spending.
2) Enjoy the float. You typically don't have to pay off a credit card until a couple of weeks after the statement date. If you use that blindly and get behind in your bills by a month, that's not good but if you use that and put the 'floated' cash to work earning interest or income in some other way, it's a free loan.
3) Peace of mind. Cash can get lost or stolen but credit cards will offer you fraud protection at no extra cost.
4) Cardmember benefits. Depending on the card and issuer, there are a number of benefits that you probably aren't aware of unless you've read the cardmembers guide. From secondary rental insurance to price

protection and damaged product replacement, there are a number of smaller benefits that you aren't going to get with cash.

5) Cash or points back. In addition to all of these other benefits, you actually are getting a discount (paid to spend money!) any time you use a card that gives you cashback or points. For most people, a card like the Fidelity American Express that gives 2% cash back is going to be the simplest and most efficient card choice but there are also cards that give rotating bonuses or that give hotel or airline points that could be even more valuable than a 2% return. The best card for you will depend on how you like to travel and where you shop but there is no reason why you shouldn't be getting at least some reward for every credit card transaction you take.

Supercharge Your Credit Card Cashback

While 2% cash back is a great way to save money on transactions with a credit card, you can supercharge your credit card bonuses by consistently getting 'signup bonuses' with new credit cards. There are many cards from Chase, Citi, American Express, Barclays, and others that offer very large and lucrative bonuses to new customers. One example of this is the $440 in travel credit that Barclays offered in 2014 for new members of its Arrival card. To get this bonus, you had to spend $3000 within 3 months but for that $3000 you spend, you are essentially getting 16% cash back. The way to really play this though is to make sure that you are ALWAYS spending against cards that are getting these signup bonuses. There are enough of these offers that if you have good credit and go slowly enough (or if you have a spouse that has good credit, you can move twice as fast), you can always be earning supercharged returns which will help lessen your overall family expenses. (For more information, search the internet for "credit card signup bonuses" or check out flyertalk.com)

Don't Pay Credit Card Fees

While it's true that some of the best credit cards often have fees, be selective about which ones you decide to keep. For us, cards fall into three categories:

1) No Fee Cards - There are plenty of great cards that don't have any fees. The Fidelity 2% cash back card, the American Express Blue Cash and Everyday cards, and Chase Freedom are all cards that have no annual fee and we keep long term. You absolutely want to have cards that you keep around for a while to help your credit score's average age of accounts.

2) Fee Cards with a worthwhile annual benefits - We keep a small number of cards that have annual fees because they have annual bonuses which have equal or more value than their fee. One example of this is Chase's Priority Rewards Club card which has a $49 annual fee but gives a free night at any IHG Property (ie Holiday Inns, Intercontinental, etc).

3) High Fee Cards - We sign up for many high fee credit cards but when we do so, they usually have a high signup bonus and have the first year annual fee waived. For these cards, we close them after ~11 months, before the annual fee hits.

By organizing our cards in this way, we avoid any annual fees except those that have a greater value than their fee. With so many credit cards and issuers, there really is no reason to pay a fee when you aren't getting fantastic value for it. Avoid the fees and let the credit card work for you!

Own Your Credit Score

Your credit score has a huge influence on many aspects of your financial life and can be one of your most valuable assets. Getting and maintaining a high credit score isn't just for people who want to rack up debt, it can play a factor in many areas including

1) Your cost of insurance.
2) How much you pay in a mortgage and whether or not you even qualify for one.
3) How much you pay for an auto loan.

4) What kinds of credit cards you are able to get - the best ones will require moderate to high income AND a high credit score.
5) In some cases, what kinds of careers you can pursue (some government positions, finance firms, and other employers may require a credit check).
Even if you never plan to take another loan, there are plenty of advantages to keeping your score in good shape.

Although the exact formula is proprietary, the basic steps to keeping your score high are
1) Pay your bills on time.
2) Keep your credit utilization low (that is, keep the amount you have charged against your credit cards much lower than your total limit). CreditKarma.com recommends that you utilize less than 30% of your revolving (ie credit cards) credit.
3) Establish a long length of credit. Keep your oldest cards open and be wary of opening too many credit cards at once if your credit history is still young.
4) Avoid too many 'hard inquiries'. Requests for new credit, whether it is a home loan, auto loan, credit card, etc generate a record on your credit report that sticks around for 2 years and has a negative effect. If you group a number of requests for the same purpose (ie mortgage applications), they may get consolidated but that isn't guaranteed. Just checking your credit score yourself though is a 'soft inquiry' and doesn't have any negative effects.

It pays to regularly check both the accuracy of your credit report as well as how your score is doing. CreditKarma.com (as well as Credit Seasme and others) offer free online credit reports and scores so you can track how you are doing.

Refinance Your Home
Although the major refinance boom of 2012 and 2013 is finished, there are still circumstances for many who may want to take advantage of

low rates. The primary reason for refinancing is to save on the total amount of interest you are paying as well as free up more monthly cash. The savings can be pretty substantial when you drop by a percentage or two on a large home. For a $300,000 mortgage, if you refinanced from 5.75% to 3.75%, your monthly payment would go from $1,750 per month to $1,389. Even more significantly, the total amount over the life of the loan that you'd pay under the first interest rate would be $630,257.96 compared to $500,163.93 with the lower rate. That's a savings of over $130,000 over those 30 years. Another benefit to refinancing is that it resets your amortization schedule which means that even if your interest rate didn't change, your monthly payment would decrease because your payment of principal is against a smaller starting amount (assuming you didn't have an interest only loan before and you have paid down principal since you got the original loan). Refinances usually come with some fees that either come in the form of fees at closing or rolled into the interest rate. Make sure you are going to stay with the loan long enough to make the fees worth the savings you get. If they do though, get ready to sign papers like crazy and then reap the savings!

Use a Discount Realtor
Buying and selling a home is a very expensive process and the largest part of this is realtor fees. If you don't need the full services of a realtor though, it may make sense not to pay full price for one. In a traditional transaction, the buyers' agent typically takes 3% and the seller's agent takes 3% as well (paid for by the seller). You can save on this though by either selling yourself or else working with an agent who will kick some of that commission back to you. If house hunting is something you are pumped up for and are already scouring listings for, you may not need a full service buyer's agent to hold your hand through selecting houses and neighborhoods, especially if this isn't your first purchase. In that case, you may just need someone to unlock a few appointments and walk you through the paperwork which is exactly what Redfin or other discount agents typically do. With the

huge numbers involved in transaction, every percentage point matters so if saving a percent or two on the transaction is possible by being a little bit more involved yourself then it may be worth the effort.

Avoid Investment Expenses

Whether you are only investing in a 401k through work or if you are investing on your own, pay close attention to fees. You are probably going to have to pay a small fee to trade stocks or to own mutual or index funds but beyond that, there really aren't a lot of great cases for further fees. Any mutual fund that has either a high load (up-front cost) or high expenses, is probably not going to be worth that expense in the long-term. In a study on mutual fund performance predictors, the research firm Morningstar found that, "Expense ratios are strong predictors of performance. In every asset class over every time period, the cheapest quintile produced higher total returns than the most expensive quintile." In other words, rather than focusing primarily on who is running the fund or what their mission statement is, focus on the expenses that are charged. High up-front or fund management fees can cost you tens or hundreds of thousands of dollars in a lifetime and don't actually benefit you with greater performance. Take a closer look at the funds in your 401k. If you don't have any low-fee options, talk with your HR about getting a better selection. If you are investing on your own, set up an account with a company like Fidelity or Vanguard where there is a large selection of low cost funds that should meet your investing needs.

Be Your Own Money Manager

There are plenty of people out there who will happily tell you what to do with your money or even handle it… for a fee. You may not naturally be very interested in looking at investment options but if you want to protect yourself and minimize fees, you don't really have a choice. Whether it is the life insurance salesperson, the annuity salesperson, the stock broker, or the timeshare pusher, they all claim to 'offer a great return' but they are all ultimately motivated by a big kickback for selling their product to you. Nobody is going to care more about helping you make and keep your money than you and you have to get at least a minimal amount of education.

There are plenty of great guides (I like, "The Only Investment Guide You'll Ever Need" by Andrew Tobias as an easy crash course) but you have to at least get to a point to understand why the simplest investment (low cost index funds) is often the best and what to watch out for. Even Warren Buffet, the Oracle of Omaha, who is famous for his active investment, preaches against 'actively' managing your money or having others do the same. In a 2013 letter to Berkshire Hathaway shareholders, Buffet said, "Both individuals and institutions will constantly be urged to be active by those who profit from giving advice or effecting transactions. The resulting frictional costs can be huge and, for investors in aggregate, devoid of benefit. So ignore the chatter, keep your costs minimal, and invest in stocks as you would in a farm." Educate yourself, take control of your own investments, and then invest for the very long term. Follow these steps and you'll avoid risking your retirement and paying for somebody else's.

Travel Savings

Understand and Use Frequent Flyer Points

Thanks to large credit card signup bonuses and hotel promotions, it has been years since we have paid anywhere close to full price for flights or hotels. The smart acquisition and redemption of loyalty points can make out-of-reach destinations possible and normal trips very inexpensive. We've found a number of strategies to be useful in our redemption planning:

1) Loyalty doesn't always pay - If you have a small amount of loyalty points and aren't playing the credit card signup game, it probably makes sense to consolidate all of your spending and travel with one hotel/airline. If you routinely are banking large credit card signup offers for points though, you probably want to consider diversifying to better protect yourself from program devaluations and to give yourself more redemption options depending on your time and destination.

2) Understand when to use which loyalty program - There are three general classes of loyalty points.

- A. Chart based redemption - These types of redemption points are the most common for hotels and airlines. There will be a chart that will determine how many points you need per night at each level of hotel, or per trip for flights. These usually don't vary by season (with some exceptions) which can make these the best deal when the cash price is high (though this is often when it is most difficult to book). These are often the best way to obtain seemingly out-of-reach redemptions like Emirates' first class flights or luxury hotels.
- B. Fixed value redemption - Southwest is the largest example of this type of loyalty program. With Southwest, each mile has a fixed value depending on the class of travel. For their cheapest class, Southwest points are worth about $0.14 each. Fixed value redemptions give you a lot of flexibility - there usually aren't blackouts and when the fare is cheap in cash price, it is

also cheap in miles, but it does mean that you will never get any extra value out of the points.

C. Credit card issuer points - Credit card issuers' points often have the most flexibility because of their set of transfer partners. Citi, American Express, and Chase all have hotel and flight transfer partners so you can hold onto the credit card points until you see a redemption you want. If you don't like putting all your eggs in one airline's basket, this is usually a great way to go. The downside (and it should be taken seriously) is that all of the credit card issuer cards that have the highest earn rate and flexibility have annual fees. For us, we usually transfer away the points and close the card before the annual fee hits but you'll have to decide if it's worth it.

3) Book Ahead - It pays to book ahead with loyalty points in a number of ways. First, some carriers (looking at you US Airways) charge huge fees to book flights with points when you do it last minute. Second, availability is tougher to rely on when you get close to your departure date. If you have your heart set on a certain flight, it may be worth it to search online for how far in advance your carrier makes flights available which in some cases is up to a year.

Hotel Alternatives

For most, hotels are the most traditional travel lodging but you can often find less expensive and more unique places to sleep if you broaden your horizons.

1) Couchsurfing - On one extreme is "couch surfing", a website and movement around offering up your space for others and accepting these offers from other strangers around the world. There is a strong social aspect and expectation for sociality but it is almost always free which is hard to beat.

2) Hostels - If you want a little more definition or reliability, there are other low cost options like hostels where you may not get a ton of privacy or your own space but you still can get a place you can count

on and at least some semblance of order that you might not get Couchsurfing. The atmosphere at individual hostels will vary greatly ranging from quiet stopping points to late night partying so do your research. Most major cities around the world have one or more hostels, usually in downtown and convenient areas. Hostels can be a great jumping off point to explore a new city on the cheap.

3) Private Rentals - Sites like Airbnb or other vacation rental companies offer another non-hotel option that works great when planning family trips small and large. It is often far more economical to rent out a house for a week when you have an extended family gathering than it would be to book a number of hotel rooms. You additionally get the benefit of full size kitchens, often washing facilities, and close proximity to the rest of your group. Even if it were to cost slightly more, all of these conveniences make this our favorite option when travelling with a larger group.

Travel in the Off Season

As much as you'd like to leave January behind and head to Cabo San Lucas or Hawaii, you are going to get a way better deal if you can handle waiting until summer. Sure these typical escape-the-winter destinations are going to be hot but they have a number of benefits going for them. First of all is fewer people. With smaller crowds and less traffic, you'll be able to spend more time relaxing and less time dealing with the bustle you tried to leave behind. Another huge benefit are the cost savings you get travelling in the off-season. Everything from flights (flying from the mainland US to Hawaii can be as low as $400 in the summer but as high as $900 in the winter), to lodging (we have consistently gotten upgrades at hotels and B&Bs during the 'off-season'), to transportation (we have gotten taxi's for half price in Mexico because no other tourists were looking to pick them up). Travelling in the off-season has downsides but for savings as great as 50%, this is a great way to keep more money in your wallet.

Avoid the Airport Taxi

Just about every major airport is located a little ways from the major city it services which often leads to a variety of transportation solutions. Although taxis take the least effort and are at times the most convenient form of transit, we've found that they cost 5 to 10 times what the mass transit option costs when available. If you are visiting a developing country for the first time, it might probably a good idea to stick with a taxi or your hotel's shuttle and not wind up hopelessly lost. For most metropolitan areas in the US, Europe, Japan, and elsewhere though, travel like a local - you are going to find convenient and dependable transportation by rail or bus that will take you downtown to where you are likely to begin your visit. Not only is this way cheaper, but it will start your trip outside the taxi/tourist bubble that is easy to fall into.

Health and Personal Care Savings

Exercise

One of the most expensive items in an individual's budget as they age can be health costs. Diseases like heart disease, cancer, and diabetes are all long term conditions that are both dangerous and expensive. Understanding the causes and cures for these and other diseases is still a work in progress but repeated studies have shown that exercise can help prevent and reduce the effects of these conditions. In addition to saving you from the pain and expense of these chronic physical conditions, exercise can give you more energy, a better mood, and better sleep, all of which will give you a better life with no expense at all!

Downsize your Gym Needs

Gyms are notorious for not being transparent with their pricing and for locking customers into plans that they don't use. While not getting exercise will certainly cost you more in the long term, paying top dollar for a gym also doesn't guarantee that you will get a better workout. First, consider gyms just a step down that offer simpler and cheaper prices. Places like Planet Fitness that offer monthly membership for just $10 are hard to beat and are going to have much of the same equipment as your typical gym which, in the US, has an average monthly cost of $55.00 (USA Today). Alternatively, consider dropping out of the gym during months that are conducive to outdoor behavior in your area. Skip the stationary bike or treadmill for the real thing and enjoy free workouts in nature.

Use Local Deal Sites

If you can't cut some pampering from your budget, consider local deal sites like Groupon, Living Social, or Amazon Local. These sites are filled with discounts from services that can afford to give a discount with the hopes of loyalty. That often includes spas, yoga lessons, hair treatments, photography, etc. You're not going to find many necessities on these sites so it is probably worth questioning the purchases but if you already know you can't go without, at least do it at half price.

Save Money on Prescriptions

If you are unfortunate to have an ongoing condition but fortunate to have prescription drugs that can help with that, being smart about your prescription choices can save you some money. A few easy options can take away some of the financial strain:

1) Opt for a 3 month refill. In one study from the University of Chicago, patients saved 29% when they got 3 month prescriptions over a 1 month option.

2) Use generic when possible. Once the patent on a drug expires and generic options are available, they are often far cheaper and nearly identical in composition.

3) Compare sources. It pays to shop around when you are getting refills. Whether it is Wal-Mart, Costco, an online source like Drugstore.com or other options, you may find large price differences between pharmacies.

4) Don't be afraid to ask for help. Talk to your doctor or pharmacist if you are in financial need. There are a number of programs that provide discounted or free prescriptions for qualified patients.

Hair Cuts without the Salon

With an average costing $28.00 for men and $44.00 for women, hair cuts can add up to a major annual expense. Since you are going to have growing hair for most of your life, consider ways that can reduce this ongoing expense. While not for everyone, one way to take a huge bite out of this cost is to learn how to cut your own or others' hair. If hair clippers will take care of most of your needs, you can easily purchase clippers for under $25 and they'll last you many years. You can educate yourself pretty easily on YouTube and with the offer of free haircuts, you'll probably have no trouble finding friends and family to practice on. If the idea of cutting your family's hair is daunting, consider either using local deal sites to pick up discounts or else finding a local cosmetology school where students in training will provide steeply discounted cuts. If you were to buy a set of clippers and use them to replace 5 years of quarterly men's haircuts, it would save you over $500 during that period.

Shampoo Alternatives

Spending $30 or more per bottle on premium shampoo and conditioner can be pretty pricey but some have found success following the 'no poo' method. These anti-shampoo followers have dropped traditional shampoo and use baking soda and vinegar to clean their hair and scalp. Dropping an expensive shampoo is not only a big money saver but its practitioners claim to enjoy a) less frequent washes, b) less packaging waste, c) fewer unpronounceable chemicals, and d) more manageable hair. There are certainly doubters but we've tried it in our house and so far have been surprisingly pleased with it.

Shop around for Glasses and Contacts

If you are lucky enough not to need glasses or contacts, be happy to skip this one. For most families though, at least one or more member of the family will need glasses or contacts. At a traditional optometrist office, you are likely to spend well over $100 on glasses with lenses or contacts. If you venture online though, there are a number of alternatives that will give you more style choices and a cheaper price. Two sites to check out are Coastal Contacts and Zenni Optical. Coastal Contacts offers $49 glasses with free shipping all the time and often you can find coupon codes that will make it even cheaper. At Zenni Optical, they have more than 30 different frames that you can get delivered under $15 ($7 frames with $5 US shipping). Either way you go, you are likely to save a bunch and you can shop at your own pace. There is the downside of not being able to see the frames on your face (unless you scouted ahead in the optometrist's office or a store) but for many the savings are worth it.

Contacts are also going to be less expensive online or at discount retailers like Costco or 1-800 Contacts. We routinely get contact prescriptions filled at Costco for 25% less than they cost at the optometrist.

Stay on the Dentist's Good Side
With most dental plans, the cleanings and preventative care are free or nearly free and fillings aren't too bad. It's the crowns, root canals and other more significant procedures that are both painful and pricey. With that in mind, it pays to spend a bit more time and money upfront and make sure to make the cleaning appointments in order to avoid the more costly repair appointments. For us, that meant spending a little bit more each month to get a package of floss picks which we are much more likely to use than a spool of floss. It also meant buying electric toothbrushes which not only are supposed to have ultrasonic benefits but also have a built in timer to force us to brush for the full recommended two minutes. By spending more upfront, we hope to have fewer expensive dentist visits later.

Be Smart About Doctor Visits
We've already talked about avoiding the doctor in the first place by exercising, and eating right will help too, but there will still be injuries and illnesses that are unavoidable. A lot of medical expense strategy will depend on your health insurance plan but some ways we have found to save money in this area include:
1) If you have a number of small questions, save them for your physical. Making a visit for every minor concern is going to cost you regardless of what medical plan you have. We prefer to just make a list and bring those questions to our regular physical. For most health plans, the yearly physical is covered anyway so make the most of it!
2) Look for the right level of attention - There are various tiers of care and associated expenses. Choosing the right one for your condition

can save you quite a bit. For us, the different tiers would be a) Ask a nurse phone line b) Doctors visit during regular hours c) Visit to an urgent care or extended hours clinic and lastly, d) Emergency room visit. If you do planning ahead of time to identify urgent care and other extended hour clinics, you may be able to avoid the costly emergency room trip.

3) Get your shots - Most health plans and many employers will offer free flu shots and other immunizations. Take advantage of those to save on future illnesses that will cost work time and potential doctor time.

4) Question tests - Make sure that you aren't getting over tested and that there aren't cheaper ways to verify a theory. Straightaway jumping to a CAT scan or treatments will cost you thousands and is not always necessary. Unless you bring it up, the doctor isn't going to consider the cost of the test but you don't always have the luxury of ignoring costs.

All of these ways to save should be balanced against prioritizing your long term health. Don't hold back from the doctor (or the emergency room) if the situation is serious. Within that though, look for ways to reduce unneeded expenses with some of the tips above.

Explore Your Benefits

This tip spans categories but can apply most readily to your health. If you are employed, especially by a large employer, you probably have a set of benefits that goes beyond just medical and retirement. For many employers, there is both an official set of benefits (which may include health insurance, a 401k, sick and vacation leave, etc) but there are also other benefits that may be included but may not be so prominent. This could include transportation benefits (free or reduced transit passes), health benefits (free or reduced gym memberships), caretaker benefit (one employer we've had provides a free sittercity.com membership), cell phone discounts, non-medical insurance discounts, retailer discounts, etc. A lot of these may not apply to you and are simply a form of advertising from other businesses but if they are relevant to you then you might as well make the most of them!

Saving with Kids

Co-op Preschool
For many under-5's, preschool can be a significant expense. The National Association of Child Care puts the cost of preschool for a year at $5,000 to $13,000 depending on where you live and how much time your child is spending there. To save on this, you could consider skipping preschool (which many child development experts don't recommend), going to a preschool that has shorter hours and less time in class, or, if you have the time and desire, consider a co-op preschool. At a co-op preschool, the parents are much more involved, typically assistant teaching once a week as well as being involved in fund raising, organizing activities, and keeping the school running. Not only will you get to be far more involved in your child's education, you'll also usually pay 50% or less of what a traditional preschool would charge. The heavy involvement isn't for everyone but if it works for you it can be financially and parentally rewarding.

Be Selective About Extracurriculars
Extracurriculars like sports, music, and clubs can be fantastic for developing confidence, social bonds and new skills. Left unchecked though, they can also be expensive, a drain of time, and stressful on both parent and child. A study by RetailMeNot found that families with children grades 6 - 12 spend an average of $671 per year on sports related costs with 21% spending more than $1000 per year. Spending this much may be a good life long investment but be selective - make sure that this is truly something the child wants and/or will benefit from. If you are only spending your time and money for a resume

boondoggle or because everyone else is doing it, you may find your wallet and nerves drained without benefit.

Avoid the New Clothes Treadmill

Kids go through a lot of clothes. They are growing fast enough you often have to do a complete wardrobe turnover every 18 months (or even more often when they are little) and they are rough enough that knees, armpits and pant-bottoms are quickly worn out. Spending full price on every new outfit you need is a surefire way to blow out your budget but there are plenty of alternatives. Our favorite non-traditional clothe sources for kids are:

1) Friends and Family - If you are from a large family or else have a broad network of friends, church members, or neighbors, you can probably get a lot of hand-me-downs for nothing. If you're lucky enough to have such an arrangement, be sure to pass the good will on!

2) Thrift Stores - We have a thrift store that we donate a lot of unneeded items to throughout the year. Although it is far from the top reason we donate, they also give a coupon for an even greater discount when you purchase items from the store. We use that, in combination with their once a month 50% off days, to make for some pretty great deals.

3) Yard Sales - We don't usually go out of our way to find garage sales but if we see one on our daily walks around the neighborhood we'll stop by. The value you'll find at a garage sale will vary wildly so be sure you know what a good deal is when you're buying. Also remember that the price at garage sales is usually pretty negotiable.

4) Consignment Stores - Consignment stores are probably our least favorite discount option but they could still be a good deal for some. In our experience, the prices are usually high enough that they aren't much better than a good sale at regular stores. If you've got a place that works for you though, and particularly if you also sell items through consignment, you can add this into your kid shopping mix.

Babysitting On The Cheap

According to the USA Today, the average cost for babysitters across the US was $10 an hour. For many couples who would love to have a night off each week (or each month!) the cost of a babysitter (in addition to any other entertainment costs) really puts a damper on things. A few ideas that may help to allow for more freedom from kids but not put the kids' college fund in jeopardy are:

1) Consider setting up a kid swap with one or more other families. If you know and trust other families with kids close to the same age, set up a trade system where you watch their kids for a night and they reciprocate. If the kids get along, not only are they not going to dread getting 'abandoned' but it can actually be less work on your part since the kids will entertain themselves.

2) Give your older children responsibility. One idea that we liked and look forward to implementing is to allow an older sibling to take the role of parent for the night. The real parents get to hide in a bedroom or another floor to watch a movie and get away while the older sibling is in charge of entertaining the younger ones, potentially preparing a meal, and then putting kids to bed. This allows you to start them babysitting a bit earlier than you normally would (since you'll be home in case things really go wrong) and also gives your child the feeling of trust and responsibility.

3) Similar to (2), if you know of babysitters that are too young for you to trust independently, see if they and their family would be willing to watch your children at their house. This gives you the backup of having another adult in the house but with the attention (and cost) that a younger babysitter would provide. It gives you peace of mind and a young babysitter the chance to get some training before they are on their own.

4) Take advantage of school and sport nights. Our child's gymnastics group regularly offers nights where parents can drop their kids off for extra gymnastics and pick them up a few hours later. The cost at first seemed high but when compared to the cost of hiring a babysitter, it actually came out to be less per hour and gave our child something

more entertaining than being stuck at home. Treat evening school activities and extracurriculars as not just a chore but a chance to have a date or spend individual time with another child.

Plan Carefully for College

For children going to college, this can be a major expense often shared by both child and parent alike. Making financially smart choices for college can help a child avoid decades of interest on student loans or spare parents money that could go to retirement. Some ideas to help reduce that financial burden include:

1) Apply for financial aid - Both through the school you choose and the Free Application for Federal Student Aid (FAFSA), you should apply every year for financial aid. Most students (60%) receive some type of financial aid which could contribute to some or nearly all of your tuition.

2) Know how aid is calculated - The income of parents and the child will be considered when determining how much the Expected Family Contribution (EFC) will be. In addition to income, assets are also considered but not uniformly. Retirement accounts, home equity, insurance policies and business equity are all excluded from the federal calculations though they may not be for a specific school.

3) Get a good 529 - The growth of investments in a 529 account will be tax free so it pays to set one up early and regularly contribute to it. Make sure that you have a low fee account with broad investment choices. Our personal favorite is the Utah Educational Savings Program which primarily uses Vanguard investments and has rock bottom fees.

4) Consider alternatives to the traditional 4-year experience. Beginning your undergraduate work at a community college or another smaller institution can often be much less expensive but, if all of the credit transfers go through, not set you back any time against a degree at a full 4 year school. Another option is to consider getting more and longer internships, particularly if they are paid. Internships make great industry connections that often lead to jobs after college. The income

from an internship can also contribute towards the next semester's fees. Even if longer internships end up pushing you back 6 months or a year for graduation, the income and networking may be worth it.

Saving with Infants

Birth Options
While more than 98% of births occur at a hospital (cdc.gov), that certainly isn't the only way to deliver and it is worth considering other options. While hospital births dominate the stats right now, just 100 years ago they were the minority and since 2004, the number of non-hospital births have been slowly but steadily increasing. Why would people choose to give birth outside a hospital? For most, it isn't just a financial choice but a choice to have a more natural and less invasive experience than you would get at a hospital. Planned at-home births or births at a birthing center are typically much more focused on the mother and the birth experience and recognize that this is just as much an emotional experience as it is a physical one. Birthing centers often have the fallback option of a hospital very close by which can give comfort for the uncommon cases where one is required. Most of these non-traditional births have very low intervention rates (correlation, not necessarily causation), and the whole process is often far less intense and expensive than going through this experience at a hospital. From birthcenters.org, "In 2011, the average Medicare/Medicaid facility services reimbursement for an uncomplicated vaginal birth in a hospital was $3,998, compared with $1,907 in birth centers." For half the price and a good chance of an improved experience, it's no surprise this is an option getting increased attention.

Diapers on the Cheap
The cost of disposable diapers for a child's first year can easily top $800 and that cost isn't likely to go down by much until the child is

potty trained. That can put a pretty huge dent in new parents' budget but there are a few options. If you are committed to disposables, Amazon's Subscribe & Save program with Amazon Mom offers 20% off diapers which includes free shipping. That kind of savings on the product as well as saving on time and gas can be a big benefit. If savings is your top priority, consider cloth diapering. Cloth diapering is coming back in style and while it is a bit more maintenance than disposables, if you are using flushable inserts then you can avoid some of the most unpleasant aspects. Even if you have to spend all of the up-front costs to buy the diaper covers and liners, cloth diapers will easily save you hundreds in your first year. If you buy used covers or can use your cloth diapers for additional years or future children, the savings only grow. For us, we tried cloth diapers for months and while we liked it, we could never find a solution that didn't cause some irritation on our child's skin (though our case was probably uncommon). If it works for you though, the savings smell sweet.

Make Your Own Baby Food
It may sound kind of strange but one of our favorite activities when we had babies was to make baby food for them. We loved the opportunity to know just what we were feeding our babies and make healthy and tasty combinations. It also helped that they seemed to almost never say no to the things we tried... if only that didn't change! Making your own baby food has a number of advantages over store-bought. First, as mentioned, is the ability to know exactly what is going into your baby. Second is the cost savings - buying fresh seasonal produce and making your own baby food is going to be far cheaper than store bought food. For us, we made organic baby food for under $0.50 per serving. Store bought organic baby food was between $0.75 and $1.00 per serving which means you are saving 25% to 50% by making it yourself. The last benefit for us was easy storage. We would make a batch of baby food and then freeze cubes of it in silicone trays. This would allow us to defrost and warm just as much as we needed without waste and without the need to waste a ton of jars. You can easily make

a week's worth of meals in under an hour on a weekend and for us, this was a money-saving no-brainer.

Don't Go Overboard

For new parents, the arrival of a baby can mean normal budget and savings habits go out the window (along with sleep). Whether it is buying a $350 stroller or a $1000 furniture set, it is easy to let fatigue and excitement overwhelm even the most frugal. Some of the things we found to be worth spending on were:

1) Comfortable chair - Before our second child, we bought a rocking recliner at La-Z-Boy on a sale for 50% its normal price. When our baby had a rough night and we needed to rock him back to sleep, we were very happy with the purchase.

2) Rocking swing - Motor powered rocking swings aren't cheap but we found our newborn consistently got more sleep in them than any other resting place. For the child and for us, this was a great relief and made the price tag worth it.

3) White noise provider - Whether you use a fan, an old mp3 player or a purpose-built device, a white noise provider is another source of increased sleep. The top-selling book, The Happiest Baby on the Block by Harvey Karp has theories on why it works but all we know is that it worked for us.

Some of the things we found weren't worth it included:

1) Expensive furniture - Either get the furniture used and/or buy furniture that is durable and can be used throughout the child's life. Spending hundreds on furniture that you'll only use until the child is 2 is probably not worth it.

2) Most toys - Despite having dozens of toys to choose from, our kids favorite toys have been spatulas, our blender (unplugged!), pots, and homemade play-doh. Kids tastes are impossible to predict so don't spend yourself silly trying to find the perfect thing to occupy them. Give them a few options and they will get creative.

3) Paying full price for formula - When we did use formula, we got a ton of samples from the hospital and doctors as well as some high value coupons. Once those ran out, we switched to the store brand. Our kids never seemed to mind one way or another (if you are switching brands, you might try easing between the two by mixing powders, making sure to keep the formula/water ratio intact) and we saved a lot in the process. Breast feeding, of course, is also going to reduce or eliminate the cost of formula and is recommended for at least the first year.

4) Expensive strollers - We saw, and tried the massive tank-like strollers but for two kids we ended up just getting one simple jogging stroller for long walks and one $20 umbrella stroller for convenience. Somehow, the umbrella stroller has held up through two years of daily walks and multiple international trips and is small and light enough to travel by car and plane. Our kids have never complained and we don't plan to take it in a marathon so we are relieved that we didn't waste money on something that wouldn't do the job any better.

Automotive Savings

Change your own Engine Air Filter
Getting a new engine air filter is recommended every 12 months or 12,000 miles and can cost up to $49.99 for the part and service at places like Jiffy Lube. On Amazon, you can buy your own filter for under $12.00 and install it yourself for free. There are many guides on Youtube or wikihow that can show you how to make the simple swap. Total saved each year? 37.99!

Change your own Cabin Air Filter
Another simple do-it-yourself auto maintenance item is changing your own cabin air filter. The cabin air filter in sedans is usually installed through the glove compartment and changing it yourself doesn't even require you to get your hands dirty. Cost of repair at a retail auto repair shop averages $59.99, cost of the filter on Amazon for normal cars averages under $20. Total saved each year? $39.99

Lights On
Headlights and taillights burn out every couple of years but don't need to be a big deal. Rather than wait for a ticket or shell out at a repair shop to get someone to swap them for you, it's easy to do them yourself. For $10 - $20, you can buy your own bulb and and, following the instructions in your owners manual or found online, you can swap one out in under 10 minutes. One thing to keep in mind if you are changing a halogen or other hot bulb, avoid touching the bulbs with your skin as the oil left behind can contribute to uneven heating and may reduce the life of the bulb.

Live with Small Scratches
Small scratches that you get from normal car use can be unsightly but don't have to break the bank. Professional auto care places will charge $150 - $200 for a scratch repair but if you are willing to spend some

time in prepping and applying your own paint (and probably sacrifice a bit of uniformity), you can just do the work yourself. You can look up online the paint color code for your car and buy the paint online or in an auto parts store. Our last small bottle of touchup paint was under $9.00. Total saved for a scratch? Over $140!

Keep your Tires Inflated
For every 1 PSI below your manufacturer's recommendation your tire pressure is, you lose 0.3% of your gas mileage. That may not sound like a lot but if you were to consistently drive with 5 PSI too low, that could add up to over $20 per year wasted! Additional tip: most gas stations will turn the air pump on for free if you go inside the station and ask.

Skip the Roadside Assistance
Depending on what credit cards are in your wallet, you may be fine skipping out on roadside assistance from your insurance provider. Many of the upper-end American Express Cards (including the personal and business Gold, Platinum, and Reserve cards) will cover the first $50 of towing expenses. If you have any Visa, for $59.95 you'll get up to 5 miles of towing, lockout service, a jumpstart, or fuel delivery (cost of fuel not included). Just call 1-800-VISA-TOW to use the service. With the cost of roadside assistance from insurance companies as high as $4.10 per month (State Farm), even if you have a breakdown every two years you would still be saving more than $19 a year by skipping this add-on.

Skip the Rental Car Coverage
Another often overlooked credit card perk is primary car rental coverage. When you rent a car, you can either 1) Buy a collision damage waiver (CDW) from the rental company ($30 per day from Hertz for example) 2) Use your own collision damage coverage from your auto insurance policy (subject to deductible and potential premium increases in case of accidents) or 3) Use a credit card that has

primary rental car coverage in addition to your own insurance policy. Primary rental car CDW coverage means that your credit card covers the first portion of costs until your auto insurance kicks in which could save you quite a bit of money if you are unfortunate enough to have to use it. As of 2014, many of Chase's higher end cards have this benefit included. The cards offering this include the Chase Sapphire Preferred, Chase Ink Bold and Ink Plus, and the Chase United Mileage Plus Explorer and Club. Discover Escape also has this feature included with the card. American Express has primary damage coverage available but it does cost $25 per rental and you have to register in advance.

Don't Drive Dumb
It's going to sound obvious but the way you drive can have a big impact on your fuel efficiency. While hypermiling may take this to the extreme, there are a number of simple things you can remember to arrive at your destination with more fuel in your tank.
1) Don't drive too fast - It takes 20% more gas to drive at 70 mph than at 50 mph. If you aren't in a rush, then take it easy on the gas pedal.
2) Accelerate gently and let yourself coast to a stop when safely possible.
3) Instead of using your air conditioner around town, use your windows to save yourself up to 5% on your fuel economy.
4) Avoid idling. Whether it is waiting for your car to warm up, sitting at a drawbridge or traintracks for more than a minute, or any other case of long pausing, turn off your engine. Rather than idling on cold mornings, all you need to do is drive gently for 5-10 minutes says AAA.

Slow Down the Replacement Cycle
According to CNBC, before the 2008 recession, the average consumer was holding onto their vehicle for 4.6 years. Even as of 2012, the average amount of time a car is held is 6.4 years. According to Consumer Reports, the average life expectancy for new cars is anywhere from 8 to 15 years, a huge step up from what many impatient

consumers are willing to live with. Rather than lusting after the shiny paint in the dealership, think about the savings you are getting with sticking with cars longer: lower car insurance premiums, smaller or no monthly payments, smaller or no financing charges, and a lot less stress when your car gets the inevitable dings and scratches. Sticking with a car 50% longer than the average can save you more than $1,500 per year.

Just Say No at the Dealership
Shopping for a car and negotiating the price is an exhausting process and just when you are ready to get things wrapped up then dealers will pour on the pressure for even more add-ons. Credit disability insurance, service contracts, and extended warranties may all sound like decent ideas when you are worn out and they are coming from a smooth talking finance 'manager' but all of these options are way overpriced and very rarely used by consumers. What's worse, since they are often rolled into the financing then you get to pay interest on these extras for the life of your loan. Skipping these options will save you more than $1000 off your total bill.

Buy used
While the execution of buying a used car isn't as simple, the value of buying used can be. The price difference between new and used has shrunk significantly between 2008 and 2014 but buying a 3-4 year old car still seems to hit the sweet spot of reliability, value, and potentially still having some remaining warranty. A new car can depreciate by as much as 25% in its first year so why pay that new-tax yourself? Be sure to get an inspection and do your research but if you aren't at least beginning with used in mind, you are probably overpaying. As one example, a Honda Civic starts at about $18,000 for a 2014, 4 door sedan. A 2010 Honda, which easily has a decade or more of life on it, runs for just around $10,000 in good condition. Whether or not a 44% discount is worth not having the new car smell is up to you but it is

certainly the option you should begin with as you start thinking about your vehicle needs.

Optimize for the 99%

When you are buying a new vehicle, it is easy to think you need to optimize for 100% of scenarios you can think of. There may be that time you need to pick up your grandparents and their 6 suitcases at the airport and so you need that huge trunk. Or maybe you think someday soccer practice will come so you better get a minivan even when you just have one or two kids. And what about hauling stuff, you might need to get a grill from Home Depot someday so you ought to just buy a truck. While all of these may be valid once in a year occurrences, if these are rare exceptions then you are probably making a mistake in getting a much more expensive vehicle to handle all of these. You (and your wallet) may be just as happy spending the $30 to rent a truck on the once-a-year you need it or paying for an airport shuttle on an odd occasion. Optimizing your vehicle choice around the 99% of your use, and not to cover every conceivable case, could save you $3,000 to $10,000 in your initial cost as well as lower maintenance costs over time.

Don't Overpay your Insurance

If your car is already paid off, insurance may be your first or second highest cost in owning your vehicle. Here are a number of ideas to help you minimize that expense:

1) Combine your insurance policies. You can usually save 5% or more if you are combining your auto insurance with the same insurance provider as your homeowner, umbrella, or renter's insurance.

2) Be careful with kids. Insurance rates soar when putting teenagers on the policy but good student discounts are available from some.

3) Raise your deductible. Raising your insurance deductible from $250 up to $500 or $1000 can save you 10% to 30%. According to Forbes, a claim is filed for a collision once every 17.9 years for a driver. If raising your deductible by $750 will save you $240 a year, and your have to pay

that cost just once over 18 years, you would be saving $3570 over those 18 years.

4) Shop around. Particularly if you are accident free and have a good credit score then it pays to check with a couple of providers each year to make sure you are getting the best deal. Don't be afraid about premiums you have already paid - when you switch they will be refunded back to you.

Wash Your Own Car

While it isn't always practical for apartment dwellers or others without a driveway and hose, washing your own car is an easy way to save money compared to paying for someone else to do it. When you pay to have it done, you either are paying for an automatic washer that runs the risk (albeit small) of doing some damage to your car or else a hand wash where even beyond the initial price you are obligated to leave a tip. Some simple ideas for making your at-home car wash even more convenient include:

1) Only run the water when you need it. Pretty obvious but if you aren't using the water to wash, don't just let it run down your driveway. Spending the $5 on a nozzle that can turn off will easily pay for itself over the course of a summer.

2) Simplify your soap. You could pay for an expensive car wash solution but dish soap works nearly as well and you've always got it on hand.

3) Skip the custom cloths. You don't need fancy equipment for applying suds. Cut up old t-shirts or towels and you've got soft and reusable rags for washing your car. Use dry towels to dry it off.

Follow Through on Recalls

The National Highway Traffic Safety Administration estimates that 30% of vehicle recalls are not actually followed through with by vehicle owners. Driving a car that has a recall on it can be dangerous (think engine, brake, or accelerator problems in 2013-2014) or simply just expensive if you didn't know about them and have to pay for repairs on your own. With more and more electronic and computer components in vehicles, recalls aren't just limited to hardware anymore either. We had a recall for a hybrid car we owned that provided a firmware upgrade that improved efficiency and gave better gas mileage. You can search for recalls at https://vinrcl.safercar.gov/vin/ where recalls over the last 15 years are listed.

In addition to recalls, it can also pay to be aware of Technical Service Bulletins (TSB), guides provided to dealers (and available to consumers) about frequent problems for a vehicle. Searching for TSBs online can save you money by letting you know of common problems with a car you own or a used car you might buy. We had an issue with intermittent wiper blades in one of our cars and through some internet searching found that a TSB had been issued for the problem. While this didn't mean it was freely repaired by the manufacturer, it did identify to us what the fix was and with the help of a more mechanically minded friend, we were able to buy the replacement part on eBay for $12 and install it ourselves. Knowing about the TSB saved us hundreds of dollars we would have spent at a repair shop or dealership.

Plan Ahead for Road Trips
Road trips can put a significant toll on your vehicle and its occupants but a bit of preparation can save time and money on the road. Some of the preparation we do for trips includes:
1) Check fluid levels and tire pressure before you leave. You are going to want to know not only that they are topped off but if one was lower than normal use would suggest, you're going to want to know why before you put a few hundred or thousand miles on the vehicle in short order.
2) Charge your electronics before you leave and bring car chargers. If you don't have car chargers, an auto power inverter will provide you with a AC power and a regular outlet so you can charge all your

portable devices. Remember not to use this too much when the car is off or you'll drain the car's battery.

3) Make sure you have emergency supplies. Unless you are going way off road, this doesn't need to be too exotic. Jumper cables, a working spare tire, extra water, some non-perishable foods (energy bars for us), minor first aid supplies and a blanket will at least buy you some time until help arrives.

4) Meals for the trip. As a kid, I thought that getting fast food on a road trip was the best part but as I've aged I've recognized that I feel way worse on a road trip after fast food and stopping for a restaurant can be time consuming and more expensive than I'm in the mood for. By planning ahead and bringing meals with you, you can avoid stopping for too long and save money compared to a dine-in restaurant. You'll also feel better by eating healthier.

5) If you want your food hot, one option is to bring a small camp stove and heat your food at a rest area. In the time that you spend warming the food, you and your family can walk around and stretch as an added bonus.

6) If you don't like planning so far ahead as bringing your own meals or don't have the desire or room to keep things cold, consider stopping by a grocery store instead of a restaurant. You can get produce or sandwich supplies there which are going to be cheap and satisfying and not leave you feeling gross for more hours in the car.

Entertainment Savings

Cut the Cable
Many people's attachment to cable is as much a habit and emotional link as it is one of pure entertainment value. The ability to always have at least something mediocre available is tantalizing enough for people to spend at times more than $100 per month for that need. Cutting the cable will be a bit painful not just for things you really do watch but also for the realization that you have to be more deliberate in your TV watching habits. Live sports are one area where it is hard to substitute (though you can always go to a friend's house or a bar) but most every other show you watch is available a-la-carte from iTunes or Amazon. Even if you were to pay to download a show every night of the month at $1.99 per show, you'd still be saving more than $40 a month vs cable. By deliberately selecting shows that are actually worth paying for, you'll probably not be buying a show every night and will find that you have a lot more time on your hands for more activities you may find more satisfying.

Box Office at Home
A prime-time movie for two and concessions at a theater can easily top $30. Beyond the cost, you have limited food selections, no control over the people in the theater, and no ability to pause or control the start time. Sure the big screen and surround sound are great but most people's 50 inch TV at home could do many movie titles justice. Pay $5.00 for an online HD rental and another $10 for a great snack and you are still coming out at half the cost. Better yet, you can invite the whole family as the cost of admission isn't going to increase with the number of people you have with you. If you were to see a movie in a theater once a month instead of once every two weeks you'd save $180 per year.

Rent Not Buy

How many times have you watched your favorite movie? Now how many times have you watched your 20th favorite movie? Chances are, you are not going to watch most movies more than once or twice at the most. Why pay to buy something you would just watch once when you could pay a quarter of the price to rent. Rather than acquiring your own collection, just pay when needed to use the vastly superior Amazon or iTunes collection. Sure, there are a few movies you are going to watch every year so shell out the $20 for the Blu-Ray. For everything else though, save the physical space and keep your money in your wallet. Instead of buying 10 movies a year at $20 a piece, rent 20 movies for $5 each and you'll still be up $100.

Make the Library Your Friend
Sure, this one may be obvious, but if you aren't using your library then you are probably spending way more than you need to for books, movies, and audiobooks. Most library districts have become way more powerful for their patrons in a couple ways. 1) Online holds - Anytime you can think of a movie or book that you want, just get online and put it on hold and you'll get it delivered (almost always for free!) to your nearest library. 2) Digital content - While you aren't going to get many new video releases online, most libraries have a connection to Overdrive or other eBook services that you can borrow from instantly and for free. If you haven't tried the library in a while, it's definitely worth checking out. If it saves you from buying a $20 book every month, that's $240 saved per year.

Spend Less on Magazines
If you are paying more than $10 a year for a monthly magazine then you could probably do way better. Buying a year worth of Wired magazine, for example, off the magazine rack could set you back over $80. Buying from Wired directly could cost $10 - $20. Buying from Amazon or sites like discountmags.com can cost as low as $5 for a year's subscription. Even better, cut the subscriptions of magazines

you just aren't reading. If there is an issue you can't miss you can always find the articles you want online.

Get Value in Gaming

Video game usage is on the rise and for many it represents a major portion of the entertainment time and budget. As an avid gamer, I've spent plenty on games and hardware but I've found a few ways that have helped me greatly reduce the expense. Some of the ways I've found to cut my gaming budget include:

1) Become a PC Gamer - Most families already have a PC and with just a few modifications (ie replacing the graphics card with a $100 - $150 upgrade) you can have a game-worthy machine. PC gaming has a number of advantages including much more variability in game prices. With services like Steam, Good Old Games, Humble Indie Bundles, and Amazon Downloads, there are many different ways to get games and many different price points.

2) Look for Digital Sales - Sales on digital titles from some of the retailers mentioned above are usually at much deeper discounts than you would find on physical media. During the Steam summer sale (which Amazon usually matches), it isn't uncommon to find games released just a year or two ago on sale for 75% off their original price. By sticking to sales and waiting a little past the release date, you can get a couple games for the price of one.

3) Free to Play - The rise of the free to play model has has brought fantastic, AAA titles to gamers without players having to spend a dime. The hope of publishers is to get gamers hooked on the free portions of the game enough to pay for some of the premium content. Even if you do end up paying a small amount, this can be a great way to get a lot of content with little cost.

4) Games with Replayability - Spend on games that you would play for a long time or play multiple times. If you are only going to play an 8 hour games once, rent or borrow it and avoid paying for an expensive box gathering dust.

5) Buy Used - If you are going to go with console gaming, consider buying and selling used games instead of paying full retail every time. If you buy used at 80% of the cost of new and sell for 60% of the cost of new, you'll be getting through 3 games for the cost of one new game.

Compared to many other hobbies, gaming is actually pretty inexpensive and by following some of these tips, you can get even greater value from it.

Hang In, not Out

If you can avoid making every social engagement with your friends a night out, you may find the events much less stressful on your budget and it can be equally fun. Whether it is a dinner party, watching a movie, playing physical or electronic games, or just drinking and socializing, you'll spend far less on all of it when you are doing it at your own house. Sure, getting away can be part of the fun but if that is all you do every time, you may find staying closer to home to give you fewer financial regrets the next day.

General Shopping Strategies

Amazon Subscribe & Save
For the kinds of products you buy regularly (groceries, household products, personal care products, etc), Amazon offers a program called Subscribe & Save. Amazon already price matches a lot of products to places like Wal-Mart and Costco but with Subscribe & Save they also offer free shipping and a discount when you sign up (you can cancel anytime). If you have between 1 and 4 subscriptions getting delivered in a month, you get 5% off each one. Where the savings really kick in though is when you have 5 more more items and Amazon gives a 15% discount. For us, it's a convenience to get the automatic delivery but it has also given us an option to get things at a discount as well as have access to some selection (particularly with organic and other specialty items) that we can't find at our grocery store.

ShopRunner
ShopRunner is a free shipping service set up by a number of retailers to act as a competitor to Amazon Prime. With ShopRunner, when you go to checkout online, instead of paying the normal shipping there is a 'deliver with ShopRunner' option that you can choose for 2 day free shipping. Most of the retailers that ShopRunner supports are smaller but there are some larger retailers you might be more likely to use like Newegg.com, Toys R Us, Drugstore.com and even Dominos delivery. ShopRunner is priced at $79 which for most people probably isn't worth it (if you're reading this, you are trying to cut back on spending, right?) but if you have an American Express card, ShopRunner is available to you for free (https://www.americanexpress.com/us/content/shoprunner.html). Even if you don't have an American Express, ShopRunner frequently has promotions that give the service away or at a large discount.

Deal Alerts

Internet deal sites like slickdeals.net and fatwallet.com are great for finding sales and discounts but if you are someone prone to impulse buys they can be an addictive drug. On a site like slickdeals, you'll see a new deal just about every hour for something that is 'too good to pass up' and 'the lowest price ever seen!' and if you are browsing there without a purpose you can end up buying things you never actually needed or knew you wanted. The usb wifi adapter I have gathering dust in a drawer but was 'only $2!' is one of many instances I had to learn from with impulse deal buys. These sites, however, are not without a purpose even for the most frugal. One of the most useful features we've found is their 'deal alert' system. With deal alerts on slickdeals, you put in a set of keywords and categories that you are looking for (say, 'Zojirushi bread maker') and whenever there is a deal that matches, you'll be notified. This serves two purposes for those looking to save money. 1) It will help ensure you are getting a good deal on the product and that you know what kinds of deals there are regularly and 2) You are delaying the purchase which can give you time to reflect if you even need the product to begin with. I have found many times where I put a product on deal alert but find that by the time a good deal comes around, I've made do with something else and I'm not actually lacking the product in my life. Deal sites can be dangerous to a budget but use their tools and you'll come out ahead.

Avoid Extended Warranties
Retailers from Amazon to Best Buy and everyone inbetween have starting pushing extended warranties for just about any electronic or breakable product. These warranties can cost up to $50 or $100 and are one of the biggest money makers for retailers - but not for you. Often times these warranties have enough exclusions on them that even on the unlikely chance that something did happen during the useful life of the product, you may not even be covered. Rather than springing for the warranty that you probably won't use, consider a couple of warranty options.

1) Shop at places and brands that stand behind what they sell. Costco is legendary for their fantastic return policy and will take back products even after they have been opened or even after many months of use without any hassle. On the brand side, look at the reputation of the product and their actual execution on warranty claims. We have a Blendtec blender that we put through the paces and although we have had a couple of jars fail, Blendtec has been willing to send free replacements during the warranty period and has fully stood behind their product.

2) Take advantage of credit card provided warranties. As mentioned in the credit card benefits section, if you have a higher-end card, read some of the small print on your credit card's explanation of benefits to see if your issue is covered. A common benefit is an additional one year of warranty beyond a product's initial coverage.

3) Get it repaired. Whether you buy the parts and repair it yourself or find someone else to repair it, consider getting it fixed before throwing it out. A $79 to $149 iPhone screen repair sounds expensive but is minor compared to the $600 you might spend buying a whole new phone.

Author H. James Harrington observed, "Measurement is the first step that leads to control and eventually to improvement. If you can't measure something, you can't understand it. If you can't understand it, you can't control it. If you can't control it, you can't improve it." We, like many others, have found that the simple act of measuring and tracking our spending has led us, almost unconsciously, to spend less. You can measure your spending automatically with your credit card provider or online aggregator like Mint but we prefer to also keep our own record in a spreadsheet. It seemed like a hassle at first but it takes us less than a minute a day and has become an easy habit. As we continue to measure our spending, we continue to find ways to control and improve it.

Embrace Minimalism
While the commercials tell us that the modern American Dream is a 2500 square foot house, 2 cars, a boat, a TV in every room and a massive collection of books, movies, and video games, that can also be stressful and exhausting. There has long been a counter culture that embraces a 'less is more' mentality of minimalism which, as we have tried to move in that direction, have found gives us more time, money, and freedom. No other spending cut will have as large of an impact as reducing your desire for more things and embracing simplicity and freedom. Whether it is buying a smaller house, living with just one car, borrowing from the library instead of buying, keeping just a 20-hanger wardrobe, or slowing down your travel, these are all choices that give you less to maintain, less reason to spend, and more freedom from material things. Minimalism is one end of the spectrum and while we are far from being all the way at that end, adopting a more minimalist mindset in our lives had brought us a lot more contentment.

Save Your Money, Save Your Life

Saving money and cutting spending can truly lead to financial freedom.

When you look at the power of cutting expenses and combine that with the power of compound interest, then you can see the radical transformation that saving and investing can have on your life. With a few conservative assumptions (your investments start from 0, Social Security and pensions are not included, your investments earn 5% after inflation and you withdraw at a 4% rate when you retire), how long you have to work depends completely on what your savings rate is.

If you can save 5% of your gross income, you'll end up needing to work for 66 years to be completely free. Increase that to 10%, the most common finance advice given, and it will still take 51, or just over the typical working lifetime. If you start adopting a frugal lifestyle and incorporate some of the ideas written about here, could you save 35% of your income? If so, you'll only need 25 working years to reach retirement. If you start that at age 22, you'll be able to reach an early retirement at 57! Take it even further like a 50% savings rate and you'll be retired in just 17 working years.

Saving rates like that aren't going to come easily, particularly at first, but as you focus on frugality as a path to freedom, you'll feel pain less and less and liberation more and more.

Good luck on your journey!

www.ingramcontent.com/pod-product-compliance
Lightning Source LLC
Chambersburg PA
CBHW051816170526
45167CB00005B/2038